A COMPREHENSIVE GUIDE TO
DEEP
FREEZING

A COMPREHENSIVE GUIDE TO
DEEP
FREEZING

by

MORAG WILLIAMS

Hamlyn Paperbacks

© Copyright The Hamlyn Publishing Group Limited 1958
First published 1958
Thirteenth impression 1971
Revised edition 1973
Tenth impression 1977
Hamlyn Paperbacks edition 1978
ISBN 0 600 31799 4

Hamlyn Paperbacks are published by
The Hamlyn Publishing Group Limited
Astronaut House, Feltham, Middlesex, England.

Printed in England by
Hazell Watson & Viney Ltd, Aylesbury, Bucks

CONTENTS

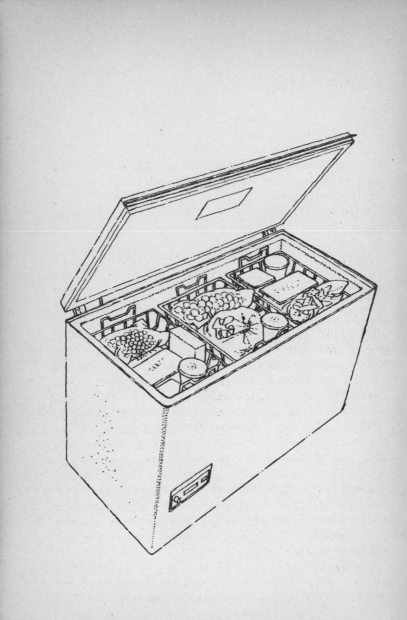

Introduction

As soon as man began to move on from a kill-and-eat existence with no thought for tomorrow, he began to devise means of keeping food.

Intelligence prompted food preservation by climatic means. The sun, where it was hot enough was used to dry; the snow to chill or freeze. Some foods, it was discovered, could be preserved by smoke or salt. Following these natural methods of preservation came the discovery that some foods could be kept in sterile jars and tins. Traditional methods have been limited, either in successful application, or because the temperature which helped to keep the foods was naturally variable, or could not be controlled. Happily, a method of food preservation has now evolved which extends to a far wider range of foods than any of the older methods; and which keeps the colour and flavour far better than any traditional method of preservation: food is stored at −18°C to −21°C and the temperature kept steady at that mark. This method is called home freezing. The term deep freezing now applies to commercial freezing of food which is done more quickly and at a lower temperature than is possible to achieve in the home.

There is very little doubt that as soon as people realise how successful home freezing can be, how many more foods can be stored by this new means of preservation, and how quick and simple it is compared to other methods, they will wish they owned a freezing cabinet.

The question of economics now enters the picture, but a standard answer is not easily available, as there are two priceless factors involved: convenience and time.

Home freezing is initially an expensive method of food preservation because of the capital outlay on the freezer, but it is undoubtedly the most successful. After the first hurdles of buying and stocking the freezer are over, this appliance, used sensibly, takes over and works for the owner. Sensible bulk buys can save pounds and life becomes less difficult – shopping can become a pleasure instead of a chore. Most women can indulge in a really big baking or cooking session when they feel like it, and store against the day when it is just another dreary task. The freezer will ensure variety in the menu and cut wastage to the absolute minimum.

Home freezing has obvious advantages for the food producer as every garden will produce its glut. The freezer owner can preserve the surplus fruits and vegetables, and have them standing by to help the menus through the months when prices rise and variety is hard to find. Meat, poultry, game and fish which cannot generally be preserved by the traditional methods can all be frozen. To the freezer owner 'out of season' can become an obsolete phrase. Those who do not grow their own food must reckon up the running costs of keeping a home freezer against the convenience of having a variety of food available and close at hand, and they can buy food when it is cheap and at peak condition.

Anyone with a young family can plan against the children's appetites and instead of baking every other day, or once a week, bake for a month. They can plan and build up for school holidays. Those who entertain can do the same and spare themselves the tiredness that so often accompanies hospitality.

There is no doubt at all that freezing has numerous advantages.

Second-hand home freezers are now coming on the market in quite large numbers; it is as well before buying any second-hand cabinet to have a refrigeration engineer check it thoroughly, or to buy from a recognised dealer in second-hand machines. Make sure that you are being sold a freezer and not a *conservator*, and that the seller can guarantee servicing. The average life of a freezer is fifteen to twenty years, so it is possible to buy a satisfactory second-hand one which will give you good service. A conservator is a cabinet for storing frozen foods only; the thermostat has been set by the manufacturers to maintain a temperature of around $-18°C$. Unfrozen food will bring the temperature in the cabinet up, and the food already stored will be brought above an even storage temperature and eventually quality will be impaired.

Types of Home Freezers

There are two types of domestic home freezers available: the top opening chest freezer, and the upright model with front opening doors.

CHEST HOME FREEZERS

Sizes range from 4·2 cubic feet to 20·8 cubic feet with *gross storage capacity* of 115 lb. to 738 lb. *Actual* storage capacities are likely to be less, for the average user will inevitably waste some space by storing irregularly shaped packages. Prices of these freezers range from about £50 to £120. The larger models have separate quick-freezing compartments for fast freezings of new food added to the frozen food store.

UPRIGHT FREEZERS

Sizes range from 1·75 cubic feet to 20·5 cubic feet, with *gross storage capacity* of 50 lb. to 749 lb. Prices range from about £43 to £218 and over. Some models have quick-freezing plates for fast freezing new additions.

Both chest and upright freezers become proportionately cheaper the larger they are, but it would be a false economy to buy a large freezer unless you can use it to the full. Prices of freezers vary so it is worthwhile comparing prices before you buy.

Both types of freezers work equally well, so the choice depends largely on individual preference. It is possible to buy a combined refrigerator/freezer but it will obviously not offer as much freezing space as either a chest or upright model. An upright freezer occupies less floor space than a chest model, but larger models should first be tried out for accessibility of stored food.

A short person may find it difficult to reach the back of the top shelves of large upright models. The most inaccessible part of the chest freezer is the bottom of the chest on the side furthest from the lock: which is worth remembering if you are 5′ 2″ or under. Most chest freezers have an arrangement of removable baskets; it is important to see whether these baskets, when fully loaded with food, are within your weight-lifting capacity.

A chest freezer loses less cold air when opened than an upright model, but this loss is unlikely to be significant for a domestic user who will not be opening and closing the lid or door more than once or twice a day.

·Remember that the weight of an upright model is very concentrated, so check if the floor is strong enough to support it when it is fully loaded. Chest models can often be placed so that they provide a working surface in the kitchen.

WHERE SHOULD THE HOME FREEZER BE PLACED?

Space and convenience will of course be the real deciders here, but the ideal place is somewhere that is dry, cool and well ventilated.

Dampness may damage the exterior and the motor. A hot room will force the motor to run harder to maintain the zero temperature.

Lack of air circulation will result in inefficient removal of heat from the condenser. Freezers should NOT be fitted tightly into an old cupboard space.

If the freezer is going to be accommodated in the kitchen,

which is the most useful place for it, keep it as far as possible from any source of heat. If it is being put into a garage or pantry, see that the chosen place is dry.

WHAT SIZE DO YOU NEED?

The choice depends on your purse, the size of your family, the likely source of food to be frozen (whether it is home-produced or bought), your entertaining, and the turnover of food in the freezer.

Because few people pack freezers with regularly shaped packets, the calculation of storage capacity is necessarily inexact. *Maximum* storage in pounds per cubic foot is reckoned by multiplying each cubic foot by 25. *Actual* storage capacity in pounds per cubic foot may not be more than cubic feet multiplied by 20. Light-weight food, such as bread, pre-cooked dishes, etc., may further reduce the actual storage capacity.

Before making the final decision, remember that it may be cheaper in the long run to over-estimate your needs than to buy a freezer that will later prove too small. You always lose a great deal when selling electrical equipment second-hand.

WHAT DOES A FREEZER COST TO RUN?

A number of factors determine running costs – the size of the freezer, its design, the number of times that the door or lid is going to be opened and for how long, efficient defrosting, careful chilling of food before it is put into the freezer and of course, electricity charges.

Each manufacturer will give a rough estimate of the current LIKELY to be consumed by his machines. It is wise to train children, and other members of the family, not to open the freezer frequently for ice cream and iced lollies, etc. The loss of cold air will cause the running costs to rise; this can often happen when the freezer is kept in the kitchen where the atmosphere is warm. If you have trouble in this direction, then keep your freezer locked!

LOOKING AFTER THE FREEZER

Each manufacturer will supply specific directions for the care and maintenance of his home freezer. The following are general directions only:

Defrosting Frost which forms round the lid or the door should be removed frequently with a plastic spatula. Frost on the walls of the freezer does not gravely affect the efficiency of the machine, and defrosting once or twice a year should be sufficient. A good rule of thumb is to defrost when the frost is between $\frac{1}{4}$ and $\frac{1}{2}$ an inch thick. If possible, defrost and clean the freezer when stocks are low.

Remove the food from the freezer and put it as compactly as possible in the refrigerator, or wrap it in layers of newspaper and put in the coolest place available.

Turn off the current and scrape off the frost with a plastic spatula. ON NO ACCOUNT SHOULD SHARP TOOLS OR WIRE BRUSHES BE USED.

If the freezer has no drain, line the bottom with layers of newspaper to catch the frost scrapings, or use a clean brush and dust pan. Hot water should never be run over the refrigerated surface, but when necessary, cold water may be used to accelerate melting. Before re-packing the freezer with food, set it to fast freeze and allow to run for 30 minutes to reduce the temperature inside the cabinet.

Cleaning the freezer It is convenient to clean the freezer when it is defrosted. Unless specific directions have been supplied with the machine, after defrosting wash the interior with a solution of warm water and bicarbonate of soda (approximately 1 tablespoon of bicarbonate of soda to a quart of water). Rinse with clean water and dry thoroughly. Do not use detergents, soaps or caustic cleaners.

Clean the outside of the machine with silicone polish, or according to the manufacturer's specific directions.

The motor Specific instructions will be supplied by the manufacturer. Most motors are sealed, and the general direction is to leave well alone, and contact the supplier if anything goes wrong.

Power failure Check plug, switch and fuses, and if the fault is not domestic, telephone the electricity authority and find out how long the failure is likely to last. If only for a few hours, or even a day, the food inside the freezer should survive without any precautionary action. The fuller the freezer is packed with frozen packets, the longer it will stay cool. Depending on the load and insulation, food will keep from 12 to 72 hours with the power off. Avoid opening the freezer during the power failure unless absolutely necessary. A warning device, bell or light, will indicate if the temperature in the freezer has risen too high. This could happen if the switch had been inadvertently turned off or a fuse blown, apart from there being a power failure. During a power cut, insulate with layers of newspapers and cover the freezer with blankets. It is now possible to insure the contents of your freezer against loss.

EQUIPMENT NECESSARY FOR FREEZING

After you have bought a home freezer cabinet, very little supplementary equipment other than packing materials is needed. The following list gives some useful accessories; most people will find that they have nearly everything required already.

1. A fine-mesh wire basket with a handle, or a cheesecloth bag for scalding vegetables.
2. A saucepan or steamer with lid, large enough to hold the wire basket.
3. A bowl in which the wire basket may be totally immersed.
4. A sharp knife.
5. A jug liquid measure.
6. A funnel.
7. Labelling materials.
8. Packaging materials include:

   a) Thick polythene bags and sheets which are most useful. Thin polythene is not quite thick enough to protect food, but is excellent for a first wrap.
   b) Aluminium foil – household foil is not thick enough so use a double thickness. Alternatively buy heavy duty foil which is thicker, and is meant for wrapping for the freezer. Foil punctures easily, so it is as well to wrap again in polythene. Foil dishes and bags are excellent if a little expensive; there are many different shaped foil dishes which are very good for pies, stews, casseroles, etc. and which can be taken from the freezer to the oven. However, take care as some dishes with a high acid content e.g. lemon and vinegar, will react with the aluminium. The foil bags are extremely good for vegetables,

stews and soups and some food can be thawed and heated through in them.

c) Plastic boxes of all shapes and sizes are useful, but the square shapes are easier to store and are less wasteful of space than the round shapes. Small packages can be stored in larger boxes to make them easier to find.

d) Waxed containers are also suitable, however they stain and if they are to be used again it is as well to line them with thin polythene.

What to Freeze: How Long and How Much

Nearly all food, except raw salad vegetables, can be preserved satisfactorily in the home freezer, but after allowing for the first excitement which will tempt all but the most calm and calculating to have a go at everything, it's wise to pause and think. There is a very dangerous trap called freezing for the sake of freezing.

To bring the problem down to common-sense proportions, is it sensible to freeze more of one food than will be needed to take one on from harvest to harvest? Of course it's not. Last year's strawberries in the freezer and this year's strawberries in the garden is a maddening experience, but that does not mean that it is child's play to avoid it. Crops can fail, and that may leave you with 'saved space'. The allocation of freezer space calls for more than planning – it also needs flexibility.

The *selection* of food for freezing is a major part of making the most of your home freezer, for space is always limited and valuable. There is no point in freezing gluts of fruit and vegetables that you do not like; the freezer should be used to preserve foods that all the family can enjoy. It should also be used to preserve *variety* – particularly for the season usually limited to apples and endless weeks of cabbage. With practically no extra effort (only bigger bakings to store away) the freezer can become a second pair of hands.

After deciding what you would like to have on hand out of the growing season, the next decision is one of quantity. An important detail is to pack the food in one meal quantities, to fit your family's needs and preferences.

The storage capacity of freezers depends on the packing

methods used. If all food is packed in identical packets and put in the freezer like a lot of bricks, then you are making the maximum use of freezer space; the chances are however, that you will be using different types of packets with different shapes. When considering what to freeze, keep these points in mind:

1. Freeze only the best, when it is at its best.
2. Pack in one meal quantities. Do not put food in the freezer without recording the date, and have a good idea when you mean to take it out.
3. Do not keep food in the freezer any longer than necessary.
4. Try not to re-freeze thawed food, as the quality deteriorates – although it is not as harmful as was once thought if carried out under hygienic conditions.

For example uncooked food from the freezer may be cooked and then cooled, before repacking and freezing.

Any frozen foodstuffs which have been thawed and then found to be unwanted, can be replaced in the freezer providing that there is still some ice in the pack. Under completely hygienic conditions, the following tips may be useful:

Cream may be placed in the refrigerator while still in its container, until defrosted enough to whip, etc. Pipe rosettes or decorations as required and put on a plastic tray; leave them open inside the freezer until they are firm then repack and seal, before returning them to the freezer. Pastry may be thawed in the refrigerator, again in its wrapping – until it is workable. Roll out, and make pies, tarts, etc., then re-freeze as quickly as possible. Cakes may be decorated while still frozen, and then returned to the freezer.

On the other hand there are certain foods which are risky and it is unadvisable to return them to the freezer. Shellfish are the most obvious of these, closely followed by made-up meat dishes – pâtés and pies, which can also be a danger.

Do not re-freeze any cooked dish which has been lying around in a warm kitchen uncovered, because bacteria will have formed.

HOW LONG SHOULD FOOD BE FROZEN?

Do not be misguided enough to imagine that success in freezing is measured in terms of years. Food can be kept for periods, in an appetising condition, which will vary with the type of food.

Zero temperature does *not* stop the chemical change which spoils food, it merely slows down the action. After the period of satisfactory storage of a particular food has expired (this period is called storage 'life' – see pages 89–90) it will begin to lose flavour and quality, although it will not be harmful to eat.

Admittedly, there is a point beyond which the period of storage 'life' when all frozen food, no matter what, begins to taste the same. Those who keep well within the recommended storage period will get the most pleasure and satisfaction from their frozen foods.

To put it in a different way, it is only economic commonsense to keep food in the home freezer for the shortest time necessary; a rapid turnover of food reduces the cost per pound of storage.

The Basic Rules

Like every process, home freezing has its basic rules. It does not pay to disregard them, for although the food will keep it will lose quality.

These are only general rules, supplementary rules which apply only to certain foods are listed under their respective chapter headings.

1. *Freeze only top quality products* Freezing cannot improve food, and freezer space is valuable. It is a waste to put in food of poor quality.
2. *Freeze food when it is at the peak of its quality* For example, when fruit is ripe and ready for eating in the normal way, and preferably early in its season. Over-ripe fruits and vegetables are too starchy or mushy, and unripe fruit can become bitter.
3. *Handle food destined for the freezer quickly* All fruit and vegetables begin to deteriorate the moment they are picked, and should be frozen soon after picking. This can be achieved by handling small quantities at a time.
4. *Observe the basic rules of hygiene* The food you put in the freezer must be clean.
5. *Follow the general and specific directions* Make a note of what you have done; you may find that in the future you need to adapt the directions to suit the variety of dishes you want to freeze, and the vegetables that you grow.
6. *Only use materials for packaging which are guaranteed to be moisture and vapour-proof, and resistant to cross contami-*

nation during storage at −18°*C* Any old packaging
material *may* work, but the chances are that it will not.

7. *Pack food in usable quantities* Packing in quantities
larger than those likely to be used at one meal, leads
to waste.

8. *As much air as possible must be extracted from each packet,
and then it must be carefully and completely sealed* It is
safer not to extract air with a straw as bacteria may be
introduced from the mouth. The packaging material,
the method of packing, and the seal, are trying to
protect the food from air, dehydration and cross
contamination.

9. *Label and date packets* It is a nuisance not to be able to
tell at a glance what the packets contain; and only
by dating can you hope to be able to arrange a sensible
turnover of food in the home freezer.

10. *Cool food to room temperature or below, before putting it in
the freezer* Food packets should be frozen quickly,
and for the sake of the food already stored the freezer
temperature should not be raised by adding too many
fresh packets at a time.

11. *Limit additions of food to the freezer to the quantity advised
by the manufacturer of your freezer, and use fast freeze switch.*

12. *Allow air spaces between packets added to the home freezer
for fast freezing* When new packets are fully frozen
they may be tightly stacked. Follow some general
system of storage, such as keeping all similar foods
together. Coloured polythene bags are useful for
identification.

13. *Observe suggested time limits for storage* After a certain
period of frozen storage, the period varies with the
type of food, frozen food begins to lose flavour.

14. *Keep records* Only by keeping a note of what remains
in the freezer can you hope to remove food while it is
at its best. This also guards against eating all the

favourite foods first, and against forgotten hoards.

15. *Plan freezing and menus* Plan freezing and menus so that all frozen foods are eaten by the time they are in season again.

16. *Do not let the freezer temperature rise above* −18°C Cabinets should normally be set to run at −21°C.

Packaging

All food must be packed carefully, and the package sealed before it is put in the home freezer. Much of the success of home frozen storage depends on making a suitable choice of package (carton, bag, sheet or rigid container). Make sure to use packaging material that is easy to handle and will not split, burst, leak, smell or allow odours or water vapour to escape or invade, while being stored.

WHY FOOD MUST BE WRAPPED

There are a number of hazards from which food in the freezer has to be protected:

a) Dehydration affects all food gradually, during storage; it is caused by low temperatures.

b) Food which is badly packed will suffer from 'freezer burn'. Chicken and meat show this by having grey spots on the surface. It must again be stressed that food should be properly wrapped to minimise oxidation or the exchange of moisture in the food for the air inside the freezer.

Materials should be:
1. Moisture-vapour-proof.
2. Waterproof, to prevent leakage, both of liquid and smells.
3. Greaseproof.
4. Odourless. (This applies also to sealing tape.)
5. Strong and durable.
6. Easy to handle.
7. Economical in storage space.
8. Capable of standing up to storage at $-21°C$.

PACKAGING MATERIALS

In previous sections packaging materials have been mentioned, but we will now examine them in more detail.

Rigid containers As a single purchase, the *moisture-vapour-proof plastic box container* which is constructed to stand up to zero temperature, is the most expensive form of freezer packaging material. On the other hand, with airtight snap-on seals, or by using zero-temperature sealing tape, it can be used indefinitely, and it is very economical in storage space. Such containers are very suitable for foods which can fill them sufficiently to eliminate pockets of air; that is, for small fruits packed in dry sugar, fruit packed in syrup, peas, mince, ice cream, soups, purées and sauces.

Flat waxed carton boxes with lids Used in conjunction with zero-temperature sealing tape, but without a liner; these have approximately the same uses as the rigid plastic box container. Whether waxed cartons can be used more than once depends entirely on extremely careful cleaning and conditions of storage between use. In general, re-use is inadvisable unless boxes have been lined with polythene.

Upright waxed cartons Sealed with sealing tape, these can be used for purées, soups, small fruit and fruit juices.

Waxed cartons with liners Can be used for vegetables, sliced meat, chops, fish and fruit. Only the liner need be sealed; the carton acts as a protector or overwrap.

Waxed tubs Round waxed tubs are less economical in storage space than square or rectangular containers, but those with lids that are guaranteed airtight require no sealing. They are suitable for fruit in syrup and other moist or semi-moist foods such as sauces, soups and ice cream.

Polythene bags Polythene bags, capable of withstanding $-21°C$ during twelve months of storage, are a popular and effective type of packing for the home freezer. A variety of shapes and sizes makes them adaptable for many types of food, such as vegetables, fish, fruits packed in sugar, and joints of a regular shape. *Air pockets must be squeezed out of the bags before they are sealed.* The danger of damage to bags in the freezer, either from the angular nature of its contents, or from frequent handling, may be considerably lessened by overwrapping.

Sheet wrappings There are now several on the market, and this thin film is excellent for moulding round awkward shapes to ensure the exclusion of air. It is as well to wrap again, or box the contents as this thin film of sheeting could be easily damaged in the freezer.

Rolls of polythene sleeves can be purchased now, and these enable you to make your own bags and shapes. An electric heat sealer is also now marketed which completely seals the sleeves, but an electric iron will also do the job.

Shaped containers Meat and poultry stews can be reheated for serving more easily if frozen in the shape of your casserole or saucepan. Line the container you will be using for reheating with a piece of foil large enough to cover the contents and crimp together at the centre on top. Pour in the stew, when cold open freeze until solid, remove from the pan, seal and freeze.

Sealing All packages or bags (except plastic boxes with special seals) must be sealed before going into the freezer. The following methods are used:

1. Twist seals are provided with polythene bags and are most efficient. Be careful that no sharp edges are left sticking out to damage other packages in the freezer.
2. Freezer tape, which is specially treated to remain adhesive at low temperatures is now available in many colours, as well as in transparent rolls.

Rubber bands tend to perish in the freezer and ordinary sticky tape is not successful.

PACKAGING MATERIALS TO BE AVOIDED

1. Any material which is not considered moisture-vapour-proof and equal to twelve months storage at −21°C.
2. Materials which leak.
3. Materials which rust.
4. Materials which break or may become brittle during −21°C storage. Glass and plastics which *have not been designed* for storage at −21°C fall within this group.

HOW TO PACK

Good packing and good packaging material must go together, for one without the other is quite useless. If packing technique is poor and allows air to get into the food through an ineffective seal, the results will be disappointing and displeasing.

The technique of packing is first of all, to eliminate air from the package and then by good sealing, to *keep* it out.

If air is allowed to remain in a package, desiccation of the food will take place, and there can be a change in the composition of food juices. If you find a heavy deposit of frost on the inner surface of a package taken from the freezer, you will know that you have not been successful in eliminating air pockets from the package *before* you sealed it.

Packing in sheet materials Place food to be wrapped in the centre of the sheet. Draw two sides of sheet together above the food and fold them over and over downwards, towards the food, to make a wrapping that is as tight and close to the food as possible. Fold the ends like a parcel, being sure to get them as close and tight to the food as you can, pressing out all air pockets. All folds must be sealed with freezer sealing tape.

It is as well to 'overwrap' parcel packs of angular food

27

in greaseproof paper, mutton cloth or clean old nylon stockings. The overwrap will not need an airtight fastening.
Packing in bags See that the bags are completely opened before filling.

When filling bags with a *liquid or semi-liquid* food see that this fills the corners of the bags and that no air pockets are left. It is better to use some sort of funnel for this type of food so that the top of the bag (the sealing edges) remain dry.

When filling with solid food, pack this neatly into the bag, then press out air pockets as carefully as you can.
Headspaces Liquid and semi-liquid food will expand while it is freezing, so room must be allowed for this between the food and the seal of the package. If this is not done, the contents will expand and may break the containers.

General directions for headspaces are that approximately ½-inch headspace should be left between *most* foods and the seals of their containers: ½–1-inch headspace should be left between liquids and the container seal.

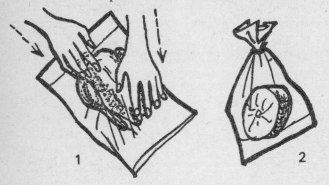

Bunched bag seal Extract air from bag by careful pressing (1). Twist the plastic-covered fastener round the neck of bag (2), turn the top of the bag down over this first twist, seal by twice recrossing fastener round the 'bunch'.

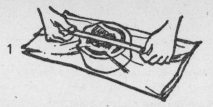

Tape-sealed sheet wrapping Lay joint on sheet. Fold two sides over meat and tape-seal down centre (1). Fold unsealed ends across package (2). Seal both ends separately, after pressing out air (3). Slip package into length of mutton cloth or clean nylon stocking (4).

Waxed cartons, unless guaranteed airtight, must be tape-sealed (5).

SEALING

Successful sealing is essential if you are to get the best results from your freezer.

The bunched bag seal A simple, inexpensive seal for bag packs is the covered wire tie-fastener.

First see that the food is packed well into the bag and that no air pockets have been left in the corners. Press out obvious air pockets. Continue squeezing bag towards its mouth bunching the unfilled part of the bag together in the left hand. With the right hand twist the neck of the bag and wind the fastener tightly round once only. Bring the top of the bag down *over* the crossed fastener, and cross the ends of the fastener tightly over this and then re-cross them. Complete the seal by twisting the ends of the fastener neatly.

Sealing lined cartons Heat-sealing linings of cartons can be sealed in the same way as heat-sealing bags. When filling, make sure that the lining is fully open and pressed into the corners of the carton. Headspace should be left when necessary. It is necessary to seal the outer carton.

Sealing unlined cartons and tubs and rigid containers Unless these have a lid which is guaranteed airtight, these must be sealed with a freezer sealing tape.

Make sure no air pockets have been left in the carton, and that sufficient headspace has been allowed for expansion. Put on lid and seal the edges completely with a continuous length of sealing tape, making sure to leave no wrinkles or folds in the tape.

LABELLING

All packets should be completely labelled and dated before they are put into the freezer. If you cannot write on the packet, stick on a label indicating the contents and the date of freezing, and cover it with a piece of sealing tape to keep it in place. Ink smudges in the freezer and it is recommended to use a felt pencil or waxed pencil (chinagraph) on labels as ordinary lead will fade after a period of low temperature storage. Write contents in legible handwriting. The pencils can be bought at any good stationers.

Do not forget that good packing with suitable materials can extend the storage 'life' of foods, but neither can offset faulty preparation, or make poor-quality food better. High-quality food, correct and speedy preparation, proper storage, and good packing are all essential. None of them should be neglected.

PUTTING FOOD IN THE FREEZER

Additions of food to the freezer should be limited to the quantity advised by the manufacturer of your freezer. They should be frozen as quickly as possible, to avoid raising the temperature in the freezer.

If the freezer has a separate freezing compartment, put new additions in this, and remove and pack closely in the general storage space when fully frozen. Air spaces should be allowed between packets of food while being frozen.

Quickest freezing is achieved by making sure that all new packets are in contact with a refrigerated surface. There is a danger, when this isn't possible or when additions of food are packed into the freezer too closely, that those in the middle may not freeze rapidly enough. Foods should reach $-18°C$ in 24 hours. This may not be achieved if, in bulk, additions to the freezer exceed one-tenth of the total capacity of your freezer. When food is frozen too slowly, spoilage may result.

Keep oven mitts handy so that you can remove frozen packs quickly and comfortably; vary container shapes to leave finger spaces between packs.

KEEPING RECORDS

All plans concerning what to freeze, and when to use the food may go awry, if they are not supported by some form of a record system The facts one has to know, not *guess at* are:

1. Where was the food put?
2. How much has been used?

One very simple method is to catalogue in an indexed loose-leaf book, or on cards. Only essential details need be recorded; for example:

		No.	Use before
Basket or shelf A	Pheasant	3̶ 2̶ 1	13/6/74
Basket or shelf B	Trout	4 3̶ 2̶ 1	9/7/74
Basket or shelf C	Raspberries	2̶ 1	6/8/74

Meat

All meat freezes well, and sometimes tender meat becomes a little more tender in storage; but do not think that the freezer is a tenderiser that will make tough meat more edible. It will not, nor can it add more flavour. It is more practical to try and soften tough meat in a stew or freeze it in a marinade.

Every inch of freezer space is valuable and costs some money, make the most of it by freezing meat of highest quality.

Many butchers now supply meat for freezing, and will by arrangement cut it into suitable joints. The meat can be bought at wholesale prices and you can ask your own butcher or the wholesaler to cut it up for you; but remember he has a living to make and will not do it for nothing.

There are many freezer shops which sell meat already packaged. This is very useful, providing that they have the different qualities clearly marked. Most of these shops have fairly competitive prices. Wholesale suppliers with ready prepared meat for the freezer are now in all parts of the country, and many will deliver to your home. Be careful about purchasing whole animals; few people are able to cope with raw flesh all over the kitchen, and butchering is a skilled trade!

General points to remember when freezing meat

1. Only 10% of the total capacity of the freezer should be used to freeze fresh food within a twenty-four hour period. This means that only half a medium-sized lamb could be done at once in a 10 cubic foot freezer. Half a pig, or a quarter of beef would need to be done over two to three days.

The temperature of the freezer will rise if more than 10% is loaded, thus slowing the freezing time and impairing the quality of the meat. Most home freezer owners are unable to store quantities of fresh meat for several days, and are really much better advised to buy meat already butchered and frozen meat to store in the freezer.

2. Meat with bones takes up precious freezer space, and bones can damage other packages. It is therefore more sensible to store boned meat in the freezer.
3. When packing your own meat, wrap carefully to exclude moisture and all air before sealing packages. Label clearly.
4. Freeze as quickly as possible, with fast freeze switch on to help lower temperature.
5. Keep a record of meat in the freezer.
6. If packing your own meat, trim off any surplus fat to save space, and guard against rancidity. Pork and bacon are the most affected, and should not be stored for too long.

CHOPS AND STEAKS

Before packing chops and steaks, consider how many are likely to be needed for each meal and apportion quantities accordingly.

Place a fold of transparent or greaseproof paper between chops or steaks before packing so that they can be separated when removed from the freezer for cooking. Press the pack tightly together to exclude air. Pack compactly in moisture-vapour-proof paper or containers and seal.

MINCED MEAT

Trim off as much fat as possible before putting meat through the mincer or buy lean minced meat. Pack mince tightly into a moisture-vapour-proof bag or carton, excluding air pockets and seal.

Mince balls may be made though it would be more economical to sacrifice the traditional shape and make them into squares and packed in usable quantities. Strictly limit the amount of seasoning, or omit it altogether and add when eaten. The addition of salt will reduce the period of satisfactory storage.

MEAT FOR STEWS

Stewing steak may have fat trimmed off, cut into cubes and pressed firmly down into a vapour-moisture-proof container. However it is more useful to prepare the meat so that it is cooked and ready to eat, except for a little extra seasoning.

One basic cook-up of stew can provide several batches with different flavours, which can be divided into family sized portions. Beef stew with vegetables, goulash, curry and a delicious dinner party dish where the meat has been cooked in wine etc. Line the serving dish with foil and freeze the mixture in the dish until hard; dip in cold water and remove shape from the dish and pack well in foil. The package can then be returned to the same dish with foil removed, heated and then served.

Do not store cooked dishes with strong spices or flavourings for long periods, but this 'batch cooking' makes menu planning for 2–3 weeks ahead child's play.

OFFAL

It is very important that offal for the freezer should be fresh, and that it should be packaged and frozen quickly.

Liver and heart may be frozen whole or sliced. If sliced,

separate the slices with two pieces of transparent wrapping, before overall wrapping. Liver should not be stored for longer than 2 3 months.

Tongue, heart and kidneys should not be stored for longer than 3 4 months.

SAUSAGES

Salt speeds up rancidity in frozen fat, therefore unseasoned, unsalted sausage meat will store satisfactorily for six months. Salted seasoned sausage should not be kept longer than one month. Frozen sausages are sold for storage in the freezer however, which have an excellent flavour.

HAMS AND BACON

There is no point in freezing hams and bacon because they keep better in cold storage, (0°C to −1°C) than in −21°C storage. In addition the 'freezer life' of hams and bacon in the piece, is limited to 2–3 months. Sliced bacon may be kept in the freezer for convenience, wrapped and sealed, but not for long. Bacon joints create problems with most home freezers as they must be used quickly because the rancidity in the fat restricts the storage time.

BULK BUYING OF MEAT

As already mentioned, this is the answer for most home freezer owners and if you are in a position to get meat at reduced price for quantity, you must remember that it will use up a large amount of space in your cabinet and can sometimes be almost an embarrassment, unless you have a large family. For myself I feel that a quarter of beef is really too much for most people, and it might be a better proposition to ask your wholesaler to select some special joints such as topside, rolled ribs and so on, and then to get these cut into the size you are likely to want. A lamb of course is a different matter, and can be dealt with in the usual joints – leg, shoulder, loin, etc. Half a pig is a good buy, and provided it is not too fat, it freezes well.

Beef and lamb have the longer freezer life – beef, 8–9 months; lamb, 6 months. Veal and pork 5–6 months.

COOKING FROZEN MEAT

Opinions have changed over the past few years on the subject of cooking meat straight from the frozen state. Many people maintain that some joints have a better flavour than if they are cooked after thawing. Pork must be cooked through, therefore partial thawing is recommended at least, but even pork can be done satisfactorily if a meat thermometer is used. This thermometer is essential if you regularly cook joints from the freezer to ensure that they are cooked right through. Adjustments must be made to the cooking times and the following times can be used as a guide:

Beef	Small joints under 4 lb. 30 minutes to the lb. and 30 minutes over.	large joints over 4 lb. 35 minutes to the lb. and 30 minutes over.
Pork	40 minutes to the lb. and 35 minutes over	45 minutes to the lb. and 35 minutes over
Lamb	35 minutes to the lb. 30 minutes over	40 minutes to the lb. 35 minutes over

It is better not to stuff meat before storing in the freezer, as this reduces storage life. Frozen chops and steaks can be cooked from the frozen state, and all meat can be allowed to thaw slowly in the refrigerator.

Fish

Only really fresh fish should be frozen, and the freezer life of fish is comparatively short. Recommended storage periods for the fatty fish, salmon, halibut, herring, mackerel, turbot, and eels for instance, are as low as two months.

Those for the lean fish, such as cod, flounder, plaice, sole, trout and whiting are about four months.

It is however, a great advantage to have a little fish in the freezer to provide variety to the menu, and a tremendous advantage to be able to store part of a salmon for most people quickly tire of eating this rich fish. The freezing of fish however, is best left to the commercial companies who produce frozen food; but if you live by the sea or have a keen fisherman in the family, you may follow this method:

1. Fish should be killed at once and put on ice until it can be prepared for the home freezer. Freeze within twenty-four hours of being caught.
2. Scale if necessary, and remove fins.
3. Gut.
4. Small fish, such as trout, may be left whole. Large fish should have their tails and heads removed, and be packed either whole or in steaks. Flat fish may be skinned and filleted.
5. Dip whole lean fish, steaks or fillets into cold salted water (1 tablespoonful of salt per quart of water) and drain. Fat fish, whole steaks or fillets should be wiped over with fresh water.
6. Pack in moisture-vapour-proof paper, carton or bag, seal and freeze. Several fillets or steaks may be packed

together to suit family needs, each piece separated from the other by two sheets of transparent film, then packed together into an overall container and sealed.

THAWING AND COOKING

Fish intended for a *slow* method of cooking may be cooked frozen or thawed. If cooked frozen, extra cooking time must be allowed. Fish intended for *rapid* cooking, such as frying should be thawed before cooking. It is advisable to partially thaw thick round fish before cooking by any method, owing to the difficulty of judging heat penetration.

Thaw all fish slowly in the refrigerator in unopened packets.

CRAB

It is really better to eat shellfish fresh, and buy commercially prepared ones for the freezer; however, here are the methods for anyone who is interested:

Start with a live crab and kill it, either by driving a skewer into the brain or dropping it into boiling water   whichever method seems the least unkind! Cook by bringing slowly to the boil in salted water, allowing 15 minutes to the pound.

Drain and cool the crab thoroughly.

Open the crab and take out any green matter, the small sack at the top of the big shell, the lungs and 'fingers', and throw all these away.

Take the edible meat from the claws and body and pack into moisture-vapour-proof bags or cartons, leaving $\frac{1}{2}$-inch headspace. Seal and freeze.

Crabs should not be stored for longer than one month.

Thaw in its container and serve while it is still very cold.

LOBSTER

Start with a live lobster and kill it according to your choice (see crab). Simmer gently in salted water, allowing 10–15 minutes to the pound. Cool and split; remove the intestines (the black line which runs down through the tail) and the sac in the head.

Remove meat from shell, and pack into moisture-vapour-proof bags or cartons, leaving ½-inch headspace.

Seal and freeze.

Lobster should not be stored for more than one month.

OYSTERS

Wash the oysters to remove dirt, then take from the shells. It is important not to lose the oyster juice; keep this on one side.

Wash the oysters in cold salted water (2 tablespoons of salt per quart of water) and drain. Pack in watertight containers, adding the saved juice. Leave ½-inch headspace. Seal and freeze.

Thawed oysters may be eaten raw or cooked. Store for not more than one month.

PRAWNS AND SHRIMPS

Boil prawns or shrimps in salted water for 3–5 minutes depending on the size. Cool in the water and then shell them. If the prawns are large enough to have a visible vein along the back, it should be removed. Cool thoroughly and pack in moisture-vapour-proof bags, again leaving ½-inch headspace. Seal and freeze.

Potted shrimps may also be packed in cartons for the home freezer, but it is important to use less seasoning than usual.

Prawns and shrimps should not be stored for longer than one month.

FREEZING COOKED FISH

Cooked fish is best frozen in a sauce to prevent it from becoming dry. Poach the fish in a little milk in a covered ovenproof dish in a moderate oven, until just firm. Do not overcook the fish or it will break up when defrosted and reheated. Flake and mix with a white or tomato sauce. Cool, pack and freeze.

Smoked fish can be frozen in boilable bags, raw with a pat of butter, or cooked.

Poultry

Now that poultry is so reasonably priced it is a great stand by in the freezer and enables the freezer owner to add even more variety to the menu.

All kinds of poultry may be frozen, and if the varieties put into the freezer are at the right stage of development, correctly killed, well packed and removed before the suggested storage limit has expired, this is one of the most successful frozen foods.

One of the greatest advantages of the home freezer is that it enables its owner to buy poultry when prices are low, or to kill surplus poultry and store for future use.

Town dwellers who own freezers will obviously buy chicken and poultry already prepared for the freezer.

Poultry can be frozen whole, or in portions or in the form of cooked dishes.

1. Starve the bird for 24 hours before killing.
2. Hang and bleed well after slaughter.
3. Pluck and remove all quills. If scalded, avoid over scalding, for this increases the chances of freezer burn. (Grey spots which can appear during storage, and are more usually caused by incorrect wrapping.) It is advisable to keep the scald between 52–57°C.
   Avoid any damage to the skin.
4. Put the bird in the refrigerator or a cool larder, for twelve hours or overnight.
5. Remove head, feet, oil sac and draw; put the giblets on one side.
6. If necessary wash and drain.

PREPARING WHOLE BIRDS

Truss the bird and tie it as for cooking. Whole birds may be stuffed before freezing, but this will limit the safe freezing period to the storage limit of stuffing (see storage chart, page 90). It is essential that stuffing should be cold before being put into the cavity.

Wrap the bird in a strong moisture-vapour-proof bag, being careful to exclude as much air as possible from the package. If there are any sharp bones, these may first be covered with small pieces of polythene, so that they do not pierce the overall wrapping.

Seal and freeze.

JOINTED BIRDS

Poultry may be frozen in joints or pieces. Broilers may be split in two along the back and breastbone; frying chickens and boiling fowl cut into sizes suited to one's needs. It is often convenient to separate the choice pieces (such as breast) or meaty pieces (such as thighs) from the bony legs, wings and backs. This may be done for separate packing and freezing, or the bony pieces may be eaten fresh, or boned for use in pre-cooked dishes – then stored in the freezer.

All joints or pieces of poultry should be washed, drained and cooled prior to packaging (unless already frozen).

Halves of poultry These should be placed together with two pieces of wrapping material between them, before overall wrapping.

Breasts or bony pieces of poultry may be placed in separate pieces of polythene with air pockets excluded or wrapped in moisture-vapour-proof material and sealed.

Giblets These are best when fresh; when frozen they have a much shorter satisfactory storage life than poultry.

Prepare giblets for the freezer by cleaning, washing, drying and chilling before wrapping. Wrap in moisture-vapour-proof material or bag, excluding air pockets. Always pack and freeze giblets separately, unless poultry packed with giblets is to be removed from the freezer within the recommended storage time of giblets. When this is planned, the giblets may be wrapped and placed within the cavity of the bird. Chicken livers are worth freezing separately as they are useful for making several tasty dishes.

Stuffing As all seasoning tends to become stronger during frozen storage, it is advisable to limit it to less than would be used in stuffings for immediate use. Pork sausage meat should not be used if the stuffing is to be placed in the cavity of the bird. The best stuffing for this means of packing is a lightly seasoned breadcrumb stuffing.

Unless a stuffed bird is being prepared for some special future event (within the storage period of the stuffing) it is advisable to pack and freeze the stuffing separately. Pack in moisture-vapour-proof material or bag, seal and freeze.

THAWING AND COOKING THE FROZEN BIRD

It is absolutely essential that poultry and game be allowed to thaw before cooking. Always allow plenty of time if you intend to have a chicken dish, as a 3 lb. bird will take 8–10 hours to thaw out at room temperature (the temperature should not exceed 16°C) and 15 hours in a refrigerator. Thawing time increases with the size of the bird e.g. a large turkey will take 2–3 days to thaw in the refrigerator. Chicken portions take about 3–4 hours at room temperature, and at least 6 hours in the refrigerator.

To retain all juices, thaw chicken still packaged.

The internal sterilising effect of heat on a chicken will not take place until a temperature of 91°C has been reached. Again, a meat thermometer is the best way to make sure that a bird is cooked all the way through.

Be sure to cook chicken or chicken pieces on a spit or barbecue thoroughly.

Cooked chicken should be placed in a polythene bag and allowed to thaw for about 9 hours at room temperature (not exceeding 16°C) and at least 20 hours in a refrigerator!

Carved poultry will thaw out more quickly, but tends to be a little dry to eat.

QUICK COOKING

Joints of poultry to be deep fried or cooked by any quick cooking method should be thawed thoroughly beforehand.

Game

Ideally, all game birds should be prepared for the freezer in the same way as domestic poultry, but this is seldom possible and often would not suit individual tastes.

The poulterer of course always freezes his game with fur and feathers on as, if he has to sell it after freezing, this is the only state in which he can do so. It is quite satisfactory from the keeping point of view, but plucking, skinning and eviscerating after thawing has been done is an unpleasant task at the best, and unless you have urgent reason for freezing this way we do not advise it.

1. Bleed the bird as soon as it is shot.
2. Keep it in the coolest place available until you get it home.
3. Hang until it is sufficiently gamey for your taste.
4. Pluck.
5. Remove as much shot as possible.
6. Draw.
7. Wash and drain cavity.
8. Wipe over body with a damp cloth.
9. Pack.
10. Cool.
11. Freeze.

It is advisable to draw any water fowl which may have been feeding on fish as soon as possible after shooting so that the fishy flavour does not extend to the flesh, but this, of course, will limit the period of hanging.

Game birds are packed for the freezer and prepared for cooking in the same way as poultry.

HARES AND RABBITS

1. Behead and bleed hares and rabbits as soon as possible after killing.
2. Hang for up to 24 hours in a cool temperature.
3. Skin and eviscerate.
4. Wash and drain cavity.
5. Wipe the carcase over with a damp cloth.
6. Cut into joints.
7. Each joint should be placed in a separate fold of paper, being careful to exclude air pockets, and then packed together into a moisture-vapour-proof container, or wrapped in moisture-vapour-proof paper and sealed.

VENISON

Anyone who is not used to large-scale jointing will find venison difficult to prepare. If a butcher is available, give him the carcase to prepare and joint, then pack the joints you wish to freeze in the same way as you would pack joints of meat. Those who cannot, or who do not wish to call in aid, should follow these directions:

1. Behead and bleed the venison.
2. Skin.
3. Eviscerate.
4. Remove shot.
5. Wash the interior with cold water.
6. Wipe exterior with a cloth which has been wrung out in cold water.
7. Prop open the belly with a stick so that air may get to it.
8. Hang in the coolest place available – ideally the temperature should be just above freezing point – for 24 hours – or until it has reached the desired condition, protecting from flies, vermin, etc.

9. Cut into joints, cutting away the flesh about the wound.
10. Pack as for joints of meat.
11. Freeze.

All game must be hung *before* freezing. If hanging after freezing and thawing is attempted, the flesh will just go bad.

Vegetables

Pick vegetables for the freezer when they are young and tender. It is a waste of time and space to wait until they become horticultural show proportions before you freeze them.

Most vegetables freeze well. The *exceptions* are radishes, raw celery, cucumbers, lettuce and similar salad vegetables. These should *not* be frozen.

1. Pick young vegetables, preferably early in the morning.
2. Wash thoroughly in cold water.
3. Cut or sort into similar sizes, rejecting all imperfect vegetables.
4. Blanch.
5. Cool in iced or running water.
6. Drain.
7. Pack and seal.
8. Freeze.

TO BLANCH IN BOILING WATER

All vegetables, except green peppers and parsley, should be blanched in boiling water or steam to retard the action of enzymes (chemical agents within the plants) which, if allowed to remain fully active, would quickly lower the quality and flavour of the vegetables during storage.

Blanch only 1 lb. of vegetables at a time to make sure of thorough blanching, and to prevent any quick change in the temperature of the water. Three to four quarts of boiling water per pound of vegetables should be allowed.

Put the washed, cut or assorted vegetables into a wire basket or cheesecloth bag and completely immerse in a saucepan of fast boiling water. Cover with a tight lid. Blanching time varies with each vegetable (see specific directions, pages 52–57), and should be counted from the moment the water comes to the boil again. If the water takes more than 1 minute to re-boil, smaller quantities of vegetables should be used unless boiling can be speeded up by increased heat under the saucepan.

Bring water back to fast boiling point before immersing another basketful of vegetables.

It is possible in an emergency to freeze vegetables during a glut without blanching, but the storage time is only two months.

TO BLANCH IN STEAM

Put sufficient water in the saucepan below the steamer to prevent it boiling dry.

When water is boiling fast, place 1 lb. vegetables in the wire basket or cheesecloth bag and lower it into the steamer. Cover with lid.

Begin to count blanching time (see specific directions, pages 52–57) from the moment steam begins to escape from the lid. *In general, steam-blanching takes half as long again as blanching in boiling water.* If blanching directions indicate 2 minutes in boiling water, steam-blanch for 3 minutes.

Steam-blanching is not recommended for leafy green vegetables such as spinach. In steam, the leaves tend to mat together.

COOLING

When blanching time is up, remove the vegetables from the boiling water or steam and immerse the wire basket or cheesecloth bag in cold running water, adding ice cubes if available. Vegetables which are not quickly cooled become mushy. Leave the vegetables in cold water only long enough to cool them through to the centre. Before being packed for the freezer they should be cooled to 16°C or lower. A general rule is to cool for the time equal to blanching time in a large quantity of water. Drain thoroughly.

PACKING

Observe the general rules of packing, choosing packet sizes that will suit your family or your dinner party needs.

BRINE PACKING

Whether to pack dry or pack in brine is very controversial. Some authorities incline to think that vegetables wet-packed in brine are less subject to toughening during storage. On the other hand, brine packing is more troublesome.

Most of the non-leafy vegetables (e.g. asparagus, runner beans, broccoli, brussels sprouts, cauliflower, peas) may be wet-packed in brine.

Prepare according to the general rules and specific directions. When vegetables have been blanched, cooled and drained, pack them in rigid containers to within $\frac{1}{2}$–1 inch of the top and then just cover with 2% cold brine solution (2 tablespoonfuls salt per quart of water). Rigid containers are better for all wet packs. Leave headspace, seal and freeze.

FREEZING

Freeze vegetables immediately after packing. If delay in doing this is unavoidable, keep the packets in the refrigerator or the coolest place available until they can be put in the freezer.

DIRECTIONS FOR INDIVIDUAL VEGETABLES

When time for only one blanching method is given, that is considered the better method.

All vegetables must be cooled and drained before packing.
All vegetable packets must be sealed.

Asparagus

Choose young, fat stalks. Avoid those that are thin and woody. Trim off inedible part of stalk and arrange spears in equal lengths.

	Boiling water	*Steam*
Small	2 minutes	3 minutes
Medium	3 minutes	4½ minutes
Thick	4 minutes	6 minutes

Beans (Broad)

Choose broad beans that are small and young. Do not wait until the outer skin is leathery. Shell.

Boiling water	*Steam*
3 minutes	4½ minutes

Pack in bags or cartons, leaving ½-inch headspace.

Beans (Runner and French)

Choose young, tender, stringless beans. Cut off ends and tips. If very small, leave whole, otherwise cut into 1-inch lengths or slice.

	Boiling water	Steam
Whole beans	2–3 minutes	3–4 minutes
Cut beans	2 minutes	3 minutes
Sliced beans	1 minute	2 minutes

Pack in bags or cartons, leaving ½-inch headspace.

Beetroot

Choose young beetroots, not more than 3 inches in diameter. Trim, then cook in boiling water until tender (25–40 minutes) taking care not to bleed them. Cool in cold water and skin. Slice or dice. Pack in bags or cartons leaving ½-inch headspace.

Broccoli

Choose compact heads with tender stalks. Discard any woody pieces, and cut to size.

	Boiling water	Steam
Thin stalks	3 minutes	4 minutes
Medium stalks	4 minutes	5 minutes
Thick stalks	5 minutes	6 minutes

When packing, arrange tips in opposite directions. No headspace is necessary.

Brussels sprouts

Choose small, tight heads. Trim and grade for size.

	Boiling water
Small sprouts	3 minutes
Medium sprouts	4 minutes

No headspace is needed in packing.

Cabbage

(Do not take freezing space for this if more interesting vegetables are likely to be available.)

Trim and shred the head of a young crisp cabbage. Blanch for $1\frac{1}{2}$ minutes in boiling water. Pack, leaving $\frac{1}{2}$-inch headspace. Frozen cabbage should not be used, uncooked, in salads.

Carrots

Choose young, or not larger than medium-sized carrots. Wash thoroughly and scale before rubbing off skin.

	Boiling water
Whole carrots	5 minutes

Pack whole, if small, or sliced or diced.

Sliced or diced carrots require $\frac{1}{2}$-inch headspace in package.

Cauliflower

Choose firm, compact heads. Trim, and break or cut into small pieces not larger than 1-inch across.

Boiling water	Steam
3 minutes	5 minutes

No headspace is needed in packing.

Corn

On-the-cob The corn must be tender and fresh. Remove husk and silk, and grade for size.

	Boiling water
Small cobs	4 minutes
Medium cobs	6 minutes
Large cobs	8 minutes

No headspace is needed in packing.

Whole-kernel Remove husk and silk. Wash. Cook cobs in boiling water for 4 minutes. Cool in cold water and drain. Cut kernels off cob, pack into containers, leaving ½-inch headspace.

Kohlrabi

Choose only young and tender kohlrabi. Trim, wash and peel. Very small kohlrabi may be left whole – others should be diced.

	Boiling water	Steam
Whole kohlrabi	3 minutes	4½ minutes
Diced	2 minutes	3 minutes

If diced leave ½-inch headspace.

Marrow

If you wish to freeze very young marrow (the size that can be eaten whole, including skin and seed) cut into ½-inch slices, or in half if they are small enough, blanch in boiling water for 3 minutes. Larger marrows should be peeled, the seeds removed, cooked until soft, and finally mashed. Both types will require ½-inch headspace.

Mixed vegetables

Prepare each vegetable according to individual directions, and combine after each has been blanched and cooled. Pack, leaving ½-inch headspace.

Mushrooms

Be sure to choose mushrooms that are fresh and free from decay. Wash thoroughly and trim stems. If mushrooms are larger than 1-inch across they should be sliced. Cultivated mushrooms need not be peeled. Mushrooms may be heated in melted butter (1 lb. mushrooms to 6 tablespoons butter) for 4–5 minutes, or until almost cooked, and cooled by putting pan in which they were cooked in cold water, before being packed for the freezer (leaving ½-inch headspace), or they may be prepared in the more usual way.

	Steam
Whole mushrooms up to 1-inch diameter	5 minutes
Button mushrooms or quarters	3½ minutes
Sliced mushrooms	3 minutes

Pack, leaving ½-inch headspace.

Parsley

Frozen parsley can only be used in stews, etc. It is unsuitable for a garnish as it becomes limp when thawed.

Wash and cut stems. Pack in small quantities. Do not blanch, but dry carefully before packing.

Parsnips

Choose small, young parsnips. Trim and peel. Cut into narrow strips or dice.

Boiling water
2 minutes

Pack, leaving ½-inch headspace.

Peas

Choose young, sweet peas. Old, starchy peas are not worth freezing. Shell.

	Boiling water	Steam
Small peas	1 minute	1½ minutes
Medium peas	1½ minutes	2 minutes

Pack, leaving ½-inch headspace.

Peppers

Choose firm, glossy peppers of uniform colour. Wash, remove seeds and stem. Slice or dice. Pack without leaving any headspace.

Peppers may be blanched in boiling water (2 minutes for slices), but if this is done ½-inch headspace must be left in the package.

Spinach

Choose young fresh spinach without heavy midribs (this rule applies to all the 'greens'). Wash very thoroughly. Blanch only a small amount at a time and agitate the container during blanching to separate the leaves and ensure heat penetration.

> Boiling water
> 2 minutes

Pack, leaving ½-inch headspace.

Turnips

Choose small, young turnips of a mild-flavoured variety. Trim, peel and dice.

Boiling water	Steam
2½ minutes	4 minutes

Pack, leaving ½-inch headspace.

Vegetable purées

These may usefully be prepared and frozen for baby foods and soups.

Cook vegetable until it is tender. Drain and cool slightly, then put through a sieve, or chop finely. Chill rapidly to 19°C maximum. The easiest method is to place purée in a basin over cold running water. Pack, leaving ½-inch head-space, seal and freeze at once.

COOKING FROZEN VEGETABLES

Frozen vegetables are like fresh vegetables, and the surest way of spoiling them is overcooking. It is, of course, particularly important to guard against this, as frozen vegetables have been partially cooked before freezing. Cook for about *half* the time fresh vegetables would take.

Boiling Most frozen vegetables may be boiled while fully frozen. The exception is corn-on-the-cob which must be completely thawed otherwise the kernels would be cooked while the cob was still a block of ice.

Steaming It is better to partially thaw all vegetables that are to be steamed to make sure of total steam penetration.

Baking Thaw the vegetables until they can be separated, and drain. Put the vegetables in a greased casserole with butter and seasoning. Cover and bake in a moderate oven, 350°F, 180°C, Gas Mark 4; 30 minutes should be ample time for most vegetables.

Frying Use a heavy frying pan that can be covered. Put 1 tablespoon butter in the pan. Melt but do not brown. Add 1 lb. frozen vegetables and cook gently until the pieces can be separated. Cover pan and cook over moderate heat until tender.

Cooked frozen vegetables may be used in the same way as cooked fresh vegetables.

HERBS

June and July are the best times to pick parsley and mint from the garden for freezing. All herbs freeze satisfactorily – rosemary, thyme, sage, marjoram, fennel. Chives freeze particularly well. When the herbs have been picked divide into small containers such as ice cube trays and freeze until firm; then pack carefully in rigid containers to store, they will keep their flavour and freshness for up to 6 months.

Fruit

An all-the-round supply of summer fruits is one of the simplest but most luxurious pleasures of freezer ownership. Fruit is very easy to prepare for the freezer, and nearly all fruit gives a satisfactory frozen result. Best results are obtained from the tart or full, round-flavoured fruits such as gooseberries, raspberries and strawberries. 'Soft'-flavoured fruits, such as pears, do not freeze so well.

Fruit needs no blanching. In general, sugar is used to retard the action of enzymes while fruit is in the freezer, though some fruits may be packed without sugar or syrup, e.g. currants, gooseberries, raspberries and rhubarb, a method which slightly shortens the period of satisfactory storage. The choice of packing method depends on the subsequent use. Fruits frozen without sugar, or frozen with dry sugar, are less liquid and therefore more useful for cooking. Fruits frozen in syrup are excellent for desserts.

1. Choose first-quality fruit, avoiding unripe fruit which will be tasteless and dull coloured, and over-ripe fruit which will become mushy.
2. Discard any defective fruit.
3. Wash fruit rapidly in water. Do not let it stand in water, but use a wire basket or colander. Be careful not to bruise.
4. Drain thoroughly.
5. Mash, slice or purée fruit destined to be frozen in this way.

6. Pack unsweetened, with dry sugar, or with syrup (see separate directions, below).
7. Seal.
8. Freeze.

UNSWEETENED OR DRY PACKING

This method is only satisfactory with fruit which can be prepared without breaking the skin, or with fruit which does not discolour during preparation. Fruit frozen by this method has a slightly shorter storage life. Place fruit on flat baking trays or plastic lids, and freeze uncovered until firm. (About 25 minutes–1 hour, depending on the size.)

Pack contents in boxes or bags, leaving $\frac{1}{2}$-inch headspace. As they are free running, a few pieces can be removed as required.

DRY SUGAR PACKING

This method is most suitable for crushed or sliced fruit, or for soft, juicy fruit whose juice draws easily.

Wash and drain fruit and prepare it as you would for the table. Put the fruit in a large bowl and sprinkle with sugar. The quantity of sugar needed varies with the tartness of the fruit, ranging from 3–5 lb. fruit to 1 lb. sugar. Mix sugar and fruit by gently shaking the bowl or stirring with a silver spoon until the sugar is dissolved. Pack into containers, leaving $\frac{1}{2}$-inch headspace.

Another dry sugar packing method is to add the sugar *during* packing. Put a little fruit in the package, sprinkle with sugar. Add another layer of fruit, then a layer of sugar. Continue in this way. The correct proportions of fruit and sugar must be observed. Seal the containers, leaving $\frac{1}{2}$-inch headspace.

SYRUP PACKING

Syrup packing is the best method for non-juicy fruits, and for fruits which discolour easily during preparation.

The strength of syrup depends on the sourness of the fruit and individual taste. A 40% syrup suits most tastes, but a weaker syrup should be used for very delicately flavoured fruit, otherwise the taste of sugar will predominate.

Syrup is made by dissolving sugar in hot or cold water, but it *must be cold before being added to the fruit.* Syrups may be prepared in advance and kept for a day in a cold larder or refrigerator.

Sugar	Water		Syrup
2 cups	4 cups	=	30% Light syrup
3 cups	4 cups	=	40% Medium syrup
4 cups	4 cups	=	50% Heavy syrup

Pack prepared fruit into containers and cover with syrup, leaving ½–1-inch headspace. It is important that fruit should be kept well down in the syrup to prevent discoloration. Place a small piece of foil or polythene over the fruit and press it down into the syrup before sealing.

All fruit packets must be sealed.

HEADSPACE ALLOWANCES

Leave headspace for all fruit packed in sugar, syrup or juice, and for pulped or puréed fruit.

Allow ½-inch for all dry packs.

For *narrow-topped wet packs* allow ¾-*inch per pint.*

For *wide-topped wet packs* allow ½–1-inch per pint.

Double headspace allowance is needed for quart containers.

DISCOLORATION

Some fruits, such as apples and peaches, are subject to discoloration or darkening during preparation, storage and thawing. There are several ways of preventing this: you can work with small quantities of fruit at speed; you can slice fruit directly into the container which has previously been partly filled with syrup; or you can slice fruit into a weak solution of lemon juice and water (juice of 1 lemon to 1½ pints water) prior to packing.

PREVENTION OF DISCOLORATION DURING THAWING

Fruits subject to discoloration benefit by rapid thawing. Fruit which has been frozen unsweetened should be put immediately into hot syrup.

It sometimes helps to put a packet of fruit which has been frozen in sugar or syrup upside down in a bowl while thawing, to make sure that all the fruit is covered with sugar or syrup during thawing.

THAWING

All frozen fruit should be thawed in its original *unopened* container.

Fruits intended for open pies, etc., must be thawed sufficiently to allow them to be spread.

Fruits for use with sponge cakes, etc., should be thawed just short of complete defrosting.

Fruits to be used with ice cream should only be partially defrosted.

Fruits to be eaten raw should have a few ice crystals left. They should be served as soon as they have reached this stage.

Thawing times	In re-frigerator	At room temperature	In basin of cool water
1 lb. fruit packed in syrup	6-9 hours	2-4 hours	$\frac{1}{2}$-1 hour

Fruit in dry sugar packets thaws rather more quickly than fruit in syrup packets. Unsweetened fruit packets take longer to thaw than syrup packs.

COOKING

Thaw fruit in original unopened container, until it can be separated, and then cook in the normal way. Water may be added if there is insufficient. Do not forget, when adding sugar, that the fruit will already be fairly sweet if it has been packed in sugar or syrup.

DIRECTIONS FOR INDIVIDUAL FRUITS

Apples

Choose firm, crisp apples. Wash, peel, core and slice.

Dry sugar pack Slice apples into a solution of salt and water to prevent discoloration (1 teaspoonful salt to 2 quarts water). Do not leave in solution for more than 5 minutes. Drain. Sprinkle sugar over apple slices in the proportion of 8 oz. sugar to 2 lb. fruit. Leave headspace.

Unsweetened pack Use the same method as dry sugar pack, but omit the sugar.

Syrup pack Make a 40% syrup (see page 62). Quarter fill containers with cold syrup, and slice apples directly into containers. Press fruit down and, if necessary, add syrup to cover. Leave headspace.

Many people prefer to blanch apple slices in boiling water for 2 3 minutes or in steam 3 5 minutes before packing by any of these methods.

Apple sauce

Cook peeled, cored and sliced apples to a pulp with a minimum of water. The best way of doing this is in a casserole in the oven. Strain off any water, and mash. Sweeten to taste and cool in a basin over cold water. Leave headspace.

Apricots

Choose firm, ripe, evenly coloured apricots. Wipe fruit but do not peel. Cut into halves and remove stones. Work quickly and with small quantities to avoid discoloration.
Dry sugar pack To prevent discoloration pour 1,000 milligrams of ascorbic acid dissolved in ½ cup of cold water over each 2 lb. of fruit. Add sugar to fruit at the rate of 4 oz. per pound, either during packing or before. Leave headspace.
Syrup pack Use a 40% syrup. Pack fruit into containers and cover with syrup. Leave headspace.

Avocados

These discolour when frozen whole. Pulp the flesh, mix with chicken stock for cold soups. Pack into containers.

Bilberries (Wortleberries)

Use the unsweetened pack if the bilberries are to be used for cooking: if to be served uncooked use a syrup pack.
Unsweetened pack Put bilberries into containers, leaving headspace.

65

Syrup pack Put bilberries into containers and cover with a
40–50% syrup. Leave headspace.

Blackberries

Avoid blackberries with large, woody pips.
Unsweetened pack Pack prepared blackberries into containers,
leaving headspace.
Dry sugar pack To each 2 lb. fruit, add 8 oz. sugar, mixing
until the fruit is well coated. Leave headspace.
Syrup pack Use a 50% syrup. Pack fruit into containers and
cover with syrup. Leave headspace.

Cherries (Sour)

Pit the cherries. The stones tend to flavour the fruit during
storage.
Dry sugar pack Add and mix 8 oz. sugar with each 2 lb. pitted
cherries. Leave headspace.
Syrup pack Make a 50% or heavier syrup, put pitted cherries
in containers and cover with syrup. Leave headspace.

Cherries (Sweet)

Red varieties are better than black for freezing. Pit the
cherries, pack them into containers and cover with a 40%
syrup. Leave headspace.

Currants (Red and black)

Top and tail currants, then wash and drain them.
Unsweetened pack Pack, leaving headspace. This pack can be
used for jelly and preserve making later on.
Dry sugar pack Use 1 part in volume of sugar to 3 parts

currants. Mix until most of the sugar is dissolved. Pack, leaving headspace.

Syrup pack Pack currants into their containers and cover them with a 40 50% syrup, depending on taste. Leave headspace.

Damsons

A tendency for the skins to toughen and the stone to flavour the fruit makes long storage impractical. It is recommended that damsons should either be stored in purée form or packed unsweetened for a short time for subsequent cheese, jam or pie-making.

Gooseberries

Select ripe berries and top and tail them.

Gooseberries may be packed unsweetened, or packed and covered with a 50% (or heavier) syrup. In either case, leave headspace.

Grapes

Select the type of grape you enjoy eating. Avoid grapes with tough skins. Cut grapes in half and remove pips. Pipless grapes may be frozen whole.

Grapes may be packed unsweetened, or packed into containers and covered with a 40% syrup. Leave headspace.

Greengages

Use method given for plums.

Loganberries

Use method given for blackberries.

Nectarines

Use method given for peaches.

Peaches

Choose fully ripe peaches. If they can be peeled without being plunged into boiling water so much the better. If not, put in boiling water for 30 seconds and then into cold water; this will loosen the skins.

Dry sugar pack Slice fruit adding sugar at the rate of 1 part in volume of sugar to each 3 parts peach slices. Mix well and pack into containers, leaving headspace.

Syrup pack Part-fill containers with 40% cold syrup and slice peaches directly into them. Press fruit well down and cover with syrup. Leave headspace.

Pears

Pears do not freeze very well as a rule. For the best results choose ripe, but not over-ripe, pears with a strong flavour.

Make a 40% syrup and bring it to the boil. Put a wire basket into boiling syrup and slice the peeled pears into this. Cook them 1–1½ minutes. Drain and cool. Put pears into containers and cover them with a *cold* 40% syrup. Leave headspace.

Pineapple

Skin and cut into slices or chunks. Throw away core.

Pineapple may be packed unsweetened, or syrup-packed in a 40% or weaker syrup. Leave headspace.

Plums

Plums (and greengages) may be frozen whole (the tendency of stones to flavour fruit will shorten storage life), or cut into halves or smaller sizes, and stoned.

Unsweetened pack Small, whole fruit may be packed into containers. Leave headspace. The skin is inclined to toughen with this method.

Syrup pack Cut and stone fruit. Part-fill containers with a 50% syrup and put fruit in containers, pressing it down and finally topping up with syrup. Leave headspace.

Raspberries

Take care not to bruise the fruit when washing, and drain carefully.

Unsweetened pack Put raspberries into the containers. Leave headspace.

Dry sugar pack Juice will run when sugar is added, so treat this as a 'wet' pack and if possible, use a rigid container. Use 1 part in volume of sugar to 4 parts berries. Either mix sugar and berries in a bowl before putting into containers, or alternate fruit and sugar (in that order) when packing. Leave headspace.

Syrup pack Use a cold 40% syrup. Pack berries into their containers and cover with syrup. Leave headspace.

Rhubarb

It is important to choose young rhubarb and freeze it early in the season   preferably before it needs skinning.

Trim and cut stalks into 1 2-inch pieces, or longer pieces if these are preferred. Colour and flavour retention are assisted if rhubarb is dropped into boiling water for 1 minute, then into cold water to cool, and drained, but this is not essential.

Unsweetened pack Pack into containers and leave headspace.

Syrup pack Put rhubarb into containers and cover with a 40 50% syrup. Leave headspace.

Strawberries

Strawberries are best frozen dry although the other methods
are possible. Two varieties of strawberries are now known
to be the best for freezing, Cambridge Vigour and Cambridge
Favourite.

Unsweetened pack Pack clean, dry fruit into containers, leaving
headspace.

Dry sugar pack Put whole, crushed or sliced strawberries into a
bowl and add 1 part in volume of sugar to every 4 parts fruit.
Mix thoroughly by tossing gently in bowl. Pack in containers,
leaving headspace.

Syrup pack Pack strawberries in container and cover with
cold 40% syrup. Leave headspace.

Fruit purées

Fruit purées are extremely easy to make and freeze. Ripe,
but not over-ripe, fruit should be used.

Trim and wash and reject any that is bruised. If the
fruit is soft enough to be put straight through a sieve or food
mill, pulp it in this way, but do not push through the 'dregs'.
Even strawberry pips are best left outside the purée.

Plums, damson, greengages, etc., should be put in a
casserole in the oven to start the juice running before being
sieved.

Mix the purée with as much sugar as you would use if
you intended to eat it at once. Pack, leaving headspace, seal
and freeze.

If a cooked purée is preferred, prepare it in the normal
way, then *cool*, pack, seal (leaving headspace) and freeze.

Fruit juices

Tomatoes Quarter washed tomatoes and put in a saucepan
over gentle heat. When tomatoes are pulped and boiling,

remove from heat and put through a sieve. Cool juice in a basin placed in cold water. Add salt to taste, pack in containers. Leave headspace and seal.

Apples Wash the apples, remove the stalks and check for scab on skin. Cut the fruit into quarters, and put into a large saucepan, allowing ½ pint of water to each 2 lb. of apples. Simmer until tender, then carefully strain the juice, cool thoroughly and pack into containers, polythene bags or plastic tubs or boxes. It can also be frozen in ice cube trays, and if this is done the frozen cubes can be knocked out and packed for storage in polythene bags. Apple skins left after using the fruit for pies can also be used for making apple juice. Add water to the peelings, simmer, then strain and pack as above. It is best not to add sugar to apple juice before freezing as it quickly starts to ferment, sweetening can always be added afterwards in the proportions required.

Apple mint While the apples are cooking add a big bunch of washed mint sprigs to the liquid, let them remain in the pan until a strong mint flavour develops, then use the juice in the same way as given above. This makes a good addition to fruit punches and other drinks.

Berry and other fruits This method can be used for any fruit except citrus ones.

Wash the fruit, checking carefully for defects or insects, mash soft fruits with a potato masher or a silver fork. Add 1 cup of water to each 4 cups of fruit. Simmer for 10 minutes, then strain through a clean cloth or jelly bag, and let it cool. Sweeten to taste, if liked, or sweeten some and leave some without sugar. Fill into any moisture-proof container, leaving ½-inch headspace. This can also be frozen in ice-cube trays and packed into polythene bags.

This fruit juice can be used for desserts, jellies, fruit drinks or just as an addition to fruit pies instead of water.

Citrus fruits Squeeze the juice from the fruits, heat to boiling point, cool quickly and then freeze. If the juice is not cooled before freezing it is apt to curdle and needs vigorously stirring when thawed.

Commercial or catering packs

It is often possible to buy large cans of such fruits as peaches and apricots or mandarin oranges, which have a short fresh season in this country, very much more cheaply than in the small sizes. You can then open the tins, divide the contents into the sort of amounts you would ordinarily use, pack into cartons and seal. Ask your grocer to get these packs for you if he does not normally stock them.

Eggs, Cream, Butter, Ice cream and Cheese

Eggs should not be frozen in their shells, because the shells will crack.

WHOLE EGGS

Break eggs into a bowl and beat. Beaten whole egg is inclined to become rather thick: to avoid this add ¾ teaspoonful of salt or 2 tablespoons of sugar to each cup of beaten egg. Note which you have done on the package.

EGG YOLKS

These will coagulate considerably unless pre-treated with 1 teaspoonful of salt, or 2 tablespoonfuls of sugar to each cup of beaten egg yolks.

EGG WHITES

Do not beat. No pre-freezing treatment is needed.

3 tablespoons yolks and whites	= 1 egg
2 tablespoons white	= 1 egg white
1 tablespoon yolk	= 1 egg yolk

PACKING

The general rule is to pack eggs in usable quantities, leaving headspace for expansion.

Small quantities of egg prepared for the freezer may be put in small bags and sealed, and a number of these bags put into a larger bag or carton.

Another method of packing usable quantities is to put the prepared eggs into a plastic ice cube tray, similar to those supplied with refrigerators. Once they are frozen, the cubes of egg may be extracted and packed in a heat-sealing bag of moisture-vapour-proof material. Each cube, or a usable quantity of cubes, may be sealed off into separate compartments in the bag with a pair of warm curling tongs or heat sealer, but be sure to put a barrier of paper between the tongs and the bag. If this method is used, it is easy to cut off the quantity of egg cubes needed, while leaving a well-sealed container which may be safely returned to the freezer.

THAWING

Thaw eggs in their unopened containers at room temperature or in a refrigerator.

Thawed egg yolks and whole eggs should be used immediately. Egg whites will keep for a day or two if they are stored in a refrigerator.

CREAM

Low butterfat cream is not suitable for freezing as it tends to separate, but cream containing 40–60% butterfat may be frozen and stored satisfactorily for periods up to 4 months.

Cream for the freezer, other than Devonshire and Cornish cream which is heat-treated in its preparation, should be first pasteurized and then cooled rapidly to 10°C. Cream should be packed in leak-proof, moisture-proof containers, leaving 1-inch headspace for expansion. It is essential that cream destined for the freezer should be prepared and frozen quickly. Cream from the top of the milk can be frozen, but for use it must be beaten and served as whipped cream.

ICE CREAM

Both bought and home-made ice cream may be stored in the freezer for 3–4 months. The better the ingredients, the longer the ice cream will retain its flavour and texture.

Store bought ice cream in its original container, making sure that it is fully frozen before being put in the freezer. It is a mistake to put in bought ice cream packages which have already begun to thaw, but if slight thawing is inevitable, wrap any carton that might leak in moisture-vapour-proof paper before putting it in the freezer.

The best home-made ice cream for the freezer is one made with pure cream and gelatine or egg yolks, and prepared in an ice cream freezer. If ice cream is made too slowly it will be grainy and will not lose this texture during storage.

Pack the ice cream in leak-proof, moisture-vapour-proof containers in usable quantities and freeze quickly.

Ice cream for parties may be put in shaped moulds, and wrapped and stored in the freezer.

Water ices may also be made and stored in the freezer.

BUTTER

Unsalted butter made from pasteurized cream will keep in the freezer for about a year. Salt butter keeps for about 6 months. Sour-cream butter will keep for only a very short period.

Bought butter may be stored in its original packing, so long as it is firm. If it is soft, the packet should be over-wrapped. Home-made butter should be packed in cartons or wrapped in moisture-vapour-proof paper.

CHEESE

Cream cheeses do not freeze satisfactorily, but hard cheeses keep well for 4–6 months providing they are correctly packed.

The blue cheeses, Danish, Roquefort, etc., are inclined to be rather crumbly after being stored in the freezer.

Allow cheese to mature to that stage of ripeness which is pleasing, or buy it at this stage. Cut the cheese into quantities which will be eaten quickly, and pack in moisture-vapour-proof paper. It is most important to observe all the rules of packing and to seal carefully to avoid drying out during storage and cross contamination.

Bread, Cakes, Sandwiches and Pastry

There is nothing to be said in favour of freezing for the sake of freezing, but there is everything to be said – and said enthusiastically – for making each baking day a slightly larger operation, so that some of its products can go into the freezer. This will extend the interval between baking days and be more economical with fuel.

UNCOOKED YEAST BREAD

Unbaked yeast breads and rolls may be frozen, but quality is inclined to vary. Unbaked yeast doughs should not be stored for longer than 5–8 weeks.

Prepare dough and allow it to rise. The dough may then be shaped or, if bulk freezing is preferred, flattened after one rising. Coating the surfaces with a good olive oil or melted *fresh* butter retards toughening of the crust. Sweetened recipes should have a little extra sugar added to them when the dough is to be frozen.

Pack single loaves in moisture-vapour-proof paper and seal. If packing a quantity of rolls, separate each layer with two sheets of transparent paper before overall wrapping with moisture-vapour-proof material and sealing.

Thawing Thaw shaped bread and rolls in a moist, warm place. The more rapid the thawing, the better the loaf. Dough frozen in bulk should be first thawed, then shaped. Put thawed bread and rolls to rise in a warm place, then bake as usual.

COOKED YEAST BREAD AND ROLLS

Cooked, frozen yeast bread and rolls store much more satisfactorily than uncooked yeast doughs.

Prepare and bake the breads and rolls according to your usual recipe. Cool as quickly as possible after baking. Wrap and seal in moisture-vapour-proof paper.

Thawing Thaw bread at room temperature.

It is best to thaw and heat *rolls* in a slow to moderate oven for 10–20 minutes according to size. Use thawed and heated rolls at once, for they become stale very rapidly. In case of emergencies it can be an advantage to have half a loaf frozen. This can then be taken from the freezer and put under the grill with the cut surface up. By the time it is toasted a slice can be cut off and toasted on the other side, while the half-loaf is again placed under the grill.

BREAD AND SCONES MADE WITH BAKING POWDER

These may be made and frozen before or after cooking. If frozen *before* cooking they should not be kept in the home freezer for longer than 2 weeks. If frozen *after* cooking storage 'life' is extended to about 2 months.

Thawing Unbaked scones and breads may be cooked in a hot oven without thawing, or partially thawed and then cooked.

Pre-cooked scones and breads may be partially thawed and then warmed up in a moderate oven.

BISCUITS

There is little point in freezing biscuits that are cooked for they will keep well in airtight tins. On the other hand, many uncooked biscuit mixtures will keep for as long as 6 months, and it is well worthwhile preparing some extra mixture for storing in the freezer.

The most satisfactory biscuit mixtures are those rich in fat but low in moisture.

Prepare the mixture and pack in usable quantities in moisture-vapour-proof material, seal and freeze.

Thawing It will be necessary to thaw the mixture so that it can be rolled and shaped. Cook in the same way as fresh biscuits.

CAKES

Cakes baked before freezing keep well for 2 4 months. Uncooked cakes should not be kept for longer than 1–2 months. Fat-free sponge cakes without icing may be stored for as long as 10 months.

Ordinary recipes may be used, but synthetic vanilla should be avoided.

ICINGS AND FILLINGS

Boiled icing and cream fillings should not be used as they crumble after storage. Egg white icings should also be avoided because they dry out. Fruit fillings will make the cake soggy. It is better to add jam to sponges after they are thawed.

The most satisfactory icing for cakes to be frozen is an uncooked butter icing made with *fresh* butter and icing sugar.

Packing Pack cooked cakes in moisture-vapour-proof material and seal. If there is any risk of breaking, put the cakes in boxes. Freeze an iced cake before wrapping.

Uncooked cake batter must be packed in a rust-proof cake tin – preferably that in which it will ultimately be cooked – wrapped in moisture-vapour-proof material and sealed.

Cooked cup cakes may be packed in a carton with a piece of transparent paper between each layer, the whole wrapped in moisture-vapour-proof material and sealed.

Thawing Thaw plain cakes – i.e. cakes without icing   at room temperature. Thaw iced cakes in a refrigerator or very cool larder and keep them there until they are served. If iced remove wrapping material before thawing.

Thaw cake batter at room temperature and cook as soon as it is thawed.

SANDWICHES

A number of fillings can be used for sandwiches that are to be frozen – sliced cooked meat, cheese, peanut butter, meat spreads and sardines, but some fillings should be avoided.

Make the sandwiches in the usual way and wrap in usable amounts in moisture-vapour-proof material, seal and freeze.

Sandwiches should not be kept in frozen storage for longer than 1 month. Open sandwiches should not be kept longer than 2 weeks.

DO NOT USE: *hard-boiled egg* because the white will become leathery; *jam* because it may seep; *crisp fillings* such as *lettuce, celery, tomato, cucumber*, because they will become soggy during storage, or when thawed; *mayonnaise or sandwich spreads containing mayonnaise* because they may curdle during storage.

BOX-LUNCHES

The freezer can be used in the partial or total preparation of box-lunches.

Separate items such as sandwiches, small cakes and fruit may be frozen and then assembled as needed.

Sandwiches and small cakes will thaw in about 2 hours after being removed from the home freezer. If *fresh* tomatoes or lettuce are available, they can be put into the lunch box when it is packed to go out, and the thawing foods from the freezer will keep them crisp and fresh.

PASTRY

For mechanical reasons, pastry dough frozen in bulk it is not very satisfactory. It takes a long time to thaw, and is inclined to crumble when being rolled. If rolled before freezing it becomes brittle during storage. The best way of storing frozen dough is in square 1-lb. packs, or rolled circles in a foil dish each separated with a sheet of foil. It is more economical to prepare complete pastry dishes for the freezer.

Apart from custard fillings, which separate, and pies covered with meringue, which toughens or dries out during storage, most standard recipes can be used for deep and shallow covered pies.

Uncooked pies Frozen, uncooked pastry usually tastes better than frozen cooked pastry. Make the pie, but do not put air vents in the top crust before freezing. For pies with pastry top and bottom, brush the inner side of the pastry with egg white to prevent juices seeping into the pastry. Wrap the pie and its plate (*which must be rust-proof and crack-proof at* $-21\,°C$) in moisture-vapour-proof material, seal and freeze.

It is unnecessary to thaw uncooked fruit pies. Unwrap them and cut vents in the top crust. Cook for about fifteen minutes longer than the time allowed for a similar fresh pie. Pies other than fruit pies should be allowed to thaw at room temperature before cooking.

Cooked pies Cook the pie in the normal way and cool it. It should be packed with its plate or dish, which must be rust-proof and crack-proof, at $-21\,°C$. Wrap in moisture-vapour-proof material, seal and freeze. Thaw at room temperature, or in a slow oven.

It is important to leave room for expansion between fruit and pastry when making a deep fruit, or similar type of pie.

Ready-cooked Foods

There is no limit to the number of emergencies for which a supply of ready-cooked food in the home freezer can be useful. Unexpected guests, harvest time, school holidays, workmen in the house, Christmas, birthdays – all the cooking preparation for these events can be undertaken in advance, so that when the time comes catering and cooking problems are minimised.

On a more everyday basis, possession of a home freezer permits planned catering to cover several weeks – bigger but less frequent bakings. Whole meals may be prepared and cooked and put into the freezer, but don't do this without some plan in mind, thinking they will come in handy one day, some day. Pre-cooked food has a short storage 'life' (see storage tables, pages 89–90). Apart from this, the shorter time pre-cooked food is stored the better, for fats tend to become rancid, and all foods undergo a gradual loss of flavour, aroma and texture. Long storage of pre-cooked food, even when it isn't dangerous, can result in food that tempts the eye but disappoints the palate.

Pre-cooked frozen food is a great field for experiment. Do not be afraid to try. Practically all cooked foods can be frozen, but some will yield a better product for the table than others. Observe these general directions.

GENERAL DIRECTIONS
1. Use good raw materials, avoiding the addition of those unsuitable for freezing.
2. Observe every rule of hygiene during preparation.

3. Do not overcook.
4. Cool thoroughly and quickly.
5. Pack and seal.
6. Label with date.
7. Freeze.

FOODS TO AVOID

1. Starchy foods such as potatoes, macaroni, spaghetti and rice in stews, soups, sauces, etc. These incline to become mushy, or acquire a warmed-up flavour when thawed and reheated. Such starchy foods may be cooked freshly and added to frozen stews and soups while they are being reheated.
2. Hard-boiled eggs. The whites become leathery during storage.
3. Mayonnaise (unless made with a whole egg in the blender) because it curdles.

POINTS TO REMEMBER

Dishes containing milk or cheese tend to separate or curdle during thawing but sometimes recombine if they can be beaten.

Fried foods become rancid quickly and tend to have a reheated flavour.

Fats tend to separate in gravies, stews and sauces. It is essential to remove excess fat before freezing.

Thickened sauces and gravies thicken still more during storage; use cornflour instead of ordinary flour as a thickening agent.

Most seasonings become stronger during storage, so should be limited, or added while reheating.

All pre-cooked foods should be used within recommended storage period.

SOUPS

Most soups freeze satisfactorily. The exceptions, which have varying results, are those containing milk or cream. Potatoes, barley, macaroni, spaghetti, rice and other starchy foods should be added to the soups *after* frozen storage; in frozen storage they become soggy.

1. Make soup, avoiding ingredients mentioned in opening paragraph.
2. Blend or strain.
3. Cool.
4. Remove all surplus fat.
5. Pack in water-tight, moisture-vapour-proof containers.
6. Leave $\frac{1}{2}$-inch headspace per pint for wide-topped and $\frac{3}{4}$-inch for narrow-topped containers respectively.
7. Seal, label and freeze.

SOUPS SHOULD NOT BE STORED FOR LONGER THAN 2 MONTHS.

Thawing Thaw clear soups in a saucepan over a low heat. Thaw cream soups in a double boiler. If a cream soup curdles, vigorous whisking or blending may restore smoothness.

COOKED MEAT AND POULTRY

The most practical cooked meat and poultry dishes for freezing are those which take a considerable time to cook. There is little point in freezing a cooked steak or chop, or a piece of fried chicken, when a better result comes from using fresh meats or freezing it raw, and only a few minutes' cooking time is required.

84

MEAT AND POULTRY DISHES WITHOUT SAUCES

Cook according to a standard recipe, but be careful not to overcook.

Minimise seasonings, or omit them altogether and add during reheating.

Remember that if meat or poultry is stuffed, its satisfactory storage 'life' is shortened to that of the stuffing.

Cool food very thoroughly.

Pack 'dry' cooked meat and poultry – i.e. without sauces and gravies – in moisture-vapour-proof paper, overwrapping if necessary, and seal.

Label and date.

Freeze.

Thawing Thaw cooked 'dry' meats in their containers.

STEWS AND COMBINATION DISHES

The quality of the frozen combination dish depends on the reaction of its ingredients to freezer storage. It is important to omit ingredients which are known to store badly. It is also important not to overcook, for most combination dishes are intended for reheating later.

Omit:

Potatoes, macaroni, rice, spaghetti and all such starchy ingredients. These do not freeze well and may be added fresh during reheating.

Hard-boiled egg. The white becomes leathery during storage.

Excessive seasoning. Seasoning becomes stronger during storage.

Mayonnaise.

Stews and combination dishes should be cooled thoroughly

and quickly, remembering that this type of food is most susceptible to attack by bacteria.

Pack stews and combination dishes in rigid (rust-proof and crack-proof at −21 °C), water-tight, moisture-vapour-proof containers, leaving 1-inch headspace. Seal and freeze. *Thawing* Dishes which are to be eaten cold should be thawed in their containers. Do this in the coolest place available. Thawing at room temperature may cause deterioration if it takes longer than 4 hours.

Dishes which require reheating may be unwrapped and reheated in the oven, or in a double boiler. It is important to restrain the heat to avoid overcooking. The oven should be low, or the water below a double boiler only warm to begin with, otherwise there is a risk of sticking.

LEFT-OVERS

If left-overs are to be frozen they must be done quickly.

Slice left-over meat and pack the slices together compactly before wrapping and sealing.

Wrap left-over cakes and tarts carefully and seal.

Put soup into a water-tight, moisture-vapour-proof container, leaving headspace, and seal.

Left-over vegetables do not freeze satisfactorily.

Left-overs which have already been in the freezer should not be refrozen.

Left-overs should not be stored for longer than 2 weeks.

SAUCES

Sauces for special dishes may be prepared and frozen, so long as the general directions are followed, and ingredients which store poorly are avoided. In general, sauces containing little fat are more satisfactory than sauces rich in fat. All excess fat must be removed before packing. When packing, remember to use a water-tight container and leave headspace for expansion.

A better result is achieved when a sauce is to be frozen if cornflour is substituted for flour in a recipe (use half the given quantity if using cornflour). Should there be any separation when reheating, whisk or stir vigorously.

Frozen Food Suppliers

Since this book was first published, a number of firms have started specialising in supplying commercially frozen food in bulk at almost wholesale prices.

The advantages of such a service to the town housewife who is not able to freeze her own home-grown produce hardly need stressing: buying food in this way not only reduces the time spent on daily or weekly shopping, but it also means considerable saving on household bills.

Most firms selling everyday fare such as meat and vegetables will also be able to supply food for special occasions; smoked salmon, prawns, scallops, asparagus and even cakes and pastries.

When choosing a frozen food supplier, it is a good idea to make sure the goods are packaged in a sensible manner. Portions of meat or vegetables should be packed in such a way that small quantities can be easily removed from the freezer.

If you have difficulty in getting in touch with bulk suppliers of commercially frozen food you can obtain details of suppliers in your area from the following source:

The Food Freezer and Refrigerator Council
25 North Row
London W1R 2BY

Storage 'Life' Tables

	Stored at $-21°C$
Bacon	2–3 months
Beef	8–9 months
Biscuits	4–6 months
Bread and scones (cooked)	1–2 months
Bread etc. (uncooked)	14 days
Butter (fresh)	6 months
(salted)	3 months
Cakes (cooked)	3 4 months
Cooked dishes casseroles, curry, goulash etc.	4 6 weeks
Crab	1 month
Cream	4 months
Duck	4 6 months
Eels	2 months
Eggs (separated)	5 10 months
Fish (fatty)	2 months
lean	4 months
Flounder	4 months
Fruit (citrus)	3 months
Fruit (non-citrus)	2 3 months
Fruit (in sugar or syrup)	10 12 months
Fruit juices (citrus)	3 months
Fruit juices (non-citrus)	10 12 months
Game birds	6 8 months
Giblets	3 months
Goose	2 3 months
Ham	2 3 months
Hare	6 8 months
Heart	3 4 months

Stored at $-21°C$

Herbs	6 months
Herring	2 months
Ice cream	3–4 months
Kidneys	3–4 months
Lamb	6 months
Left-over cooked food	14 days or less
Liver	3–4 months
Lobster	1 month
Mackerel	2 months
Mince (unseasoned)	3 months
Oysters	1 month
Pies (uncooked)	3 4 months
Plaice	4 months
Pork	5–6 months
Chicken (unstuffed)	12 months
Chicken (stuffed)	2 4 weeks
Prawns	1 month
Purées	8 10 months
Rabbit	6 8 months
Salmon	4 months
Sandwiches	1–2 months
Sauces	2–3 months
Sauces (unseasoned)	3 months
Sauces (seasoned)	1 month or less
Shrimps	1 month
Soups	1–2 months
Stuffings	2–4 weeks
Tarts	2 3 months
Tongue	3 4 months
Trout	4 months
Turbot	2 months
Veal	5 6 months
Vegetables	8 10 months
Venison	12 months
Whiting	3 4 months

Index

INDEX

The Hamlyn Kitchen Library Series

Myra Street

PASTA COOKBOOK

Long or short, fat and thin, pasta comes in dozens of forms to suit dozens of dishes – soups, salads, fish and meat savouries, even puddings. So be adventurous, delight friends and family with oodles of noodles and plenty of pasta – all inexpensive, nutritious and quite delicious.

The Hamlyn Kitchen Library Series

MARGUERITE PATTEN'S FAMILY COOKBOOK

Have fun feeding the family and friends from this host of recipes for all occasions. Whether light summer lunch or warming winter dinner, from pasta party to buffet entertaining, these dishes will fast become firm favourites with the whole family.